Catholic Poems and Letters

Given to Father Coleman my friend.

MARCH 24, 1997

David R Wehner

DAVID R WEHNER
201 KIPLING STREET
PALO ALTO CA 94301-1216

Catholic Poems and Letters

Dave R. Wehner

VANTAGE PRESS
New York

FIRST EDITION

All rights reserved, including the right of
reproduction in whole or in part in any form.

Copyright © 1997 by Dave R. Wehner

Published by Vantage Press, Inc.
516 West 34th Street, New York, New York 10001

Manufactured in the United States of America
ISBN: 0-533-12062-4

Library of Congress Catalog Card No.: 96-90468

0 9 8 7 6 5 4 3 2 1

To my dad, and my grandpa

Contents

AUGUST 29, 1995	1
SEPTEMBER 10, 1995	3
SEPTEMBER 18, 1995	5
SEPTEMBER 17, 1995	7
SEPTEMBER 24, 1995	9
MARY	11
UNDATED (I)	13
MARY OF THE MIRACULOUS MEDAL	15
A TELEVISION SET IN EVERY AMERICAN HOME	17
OCTOBER 18, 1995	19
GRACE, WORKS & MERIT	21
UNDATED (II)	23
MARY, OUR L I F E	25
NOVEMBER 11, 1995	29
WHAT WE SHARE WITH JESUS	31
MARY IS OUR HOPE JESUS OUR SALVATION	33
IMMACULATE CONCEPTION	35
MARY, A WAY TO JESUS AND HEAVEN	37
MARY STOOD AT THE FOOT OF THE CROSS	39
FOUR CATHOLIC DOGMAS ABOUT THE VIRGIN MARY	41
GRACE	43
TIME TRANSCENDED IN A MIRACLE	46
JANUARY 21, 1996	48
JANUARY 27, 1996	50
JESUS, ALWAYS PRESENT IN OUR LIVES	51
FEBRUARY 13, 1996	53

Catholic Poems and Letters

AUGUST 29, 1995

Tuesday morning
2:05 A.M.

Dear Grandpa,

We see in the Assumption of Mary, Jesus who is God, honoring His mother. This is done by not letting the body of Mary know decay in the grave. Also, in her Immaculate Conception, she was conceived free from all sin. This further shows the love and respect Jesus has for His mother.

The miraculous Medal, the one I sent you, is also known as the Medal of the Immaculate Conception. On the medal are written these words: *O Mary conceived without sin, pray for us who have recourse (turn) to thee.* This medal was given to Saint Catherine Laboure in 1830. It too shows the prominence of Mary in God's universal plan.

Pope Pius XII must have realized this when, in 1950, he proclaimed infallibly the Assumption of Mary.

So we have mother and Son. The only two perfect human beings. The mother, perfect, by two favors granted by God, and her total acquiescence every day of her life to the will of God. The Son Jesus, being both human and divine, living a perfect life on earth.

Mary of course is not God. God being: Father, Son, and Holy Spirit. But in every way she is the most special of all human beings, having led a perfect life here on earth, never giving in to the temptation of sin. Not even the Apostles are perfect as is Mary. She is queen of the universe, Queen of Heaven.

Yes, we pray to Mary, because she leads us to the Sacred Heart of Jesus. And because the grace of God flows from the Miraculous Medal. Mary can lift us to her Son when we pray the rosary. She has been in the plan of God since the beginning of time. Mother and Son are now united in heaven, the grace of God streaming forth from her hands. And we too are her children.

SEPTEMBER 10, 1995

> 11:00 P.M.
> Sunday night

Dear Grandpa,
    The gardens are overflowing with pretty, sweet,
        sweet smelling flowers.
    Birds are darting to and fro, seeking food for life.
    The great ball of fire in the sky shines mightily
        overhead.
    Little girls and boys run about at play.
    Their parents keep a watchful eye.

    This is the end of summer.
    The weather is still good outside.
    In this beautiful time of year, it's easy for me to think
    Of the Blessed Mother Mary.

    As I pray my rosary every night in my room,
    Mary enters into my heart.
    She brings with her grace from God.
    Mary is the mother of God, the mother of Jesus Christ.
    The virgin mother always leads me to Christ.
    From her comes the grace of the Spirit of Christ.

    She dispenses all the graces from the throne of God.
    O Queen of Heaven, help me to know you better.
    O Queen of the Apostles, bless me.

O Queen of the Angels, comfort me.
Our Lady of Sorrows, make me strong in my trial.

Bring to me that summer day I see you amid.
Let the children play and run about.
The birds to sing their songs.
Be my mother, dear Mary of mine.

SEPTEMBER 18, 1995

When the priest says, "This is my body, this is my blood," this is known as the separate consecration. It makes the death of Jesus on the cross known to us during the mass. This is because when the blood was separated from the body of Jesus, he died on the cross. When we receive communion however, we receive the risen glorified Christ. So the Holy Eucharist can be said to represent the death and resurrection of Our Savior Jesus Christ. And it "is" the body and blood, soul and divinity, of Jesus Christ. This then is a sacrament by which we receive great graces, and is a foundation to our salvation in heaven one day with Jesus Christ.

The Sacrament of Penance is available to us to cleanse us of mortal sin—most importantly. If we only have venial sins, we also may go to confession. If mortal sin has removed us from a state of grace, we may re-establish this state of grace through confession.

Grace comes through the Eucharist and confession. These two sacraments work hand in hand. In communion, we receive the Lord Jesus into our very being, with all his love for us, and the grace of God. The Sacrament of Penance, when used for venial sin, also gives us grace from God. It does this too when used for mortal sin; but more importantly it re-establishes connection of a cut off soul with Jesus Christ Our Lord.

The main thing I would add to these two key sacraments is a daily praying of the rosary. This is a good work done amid grace that gains us merit towards our salvation in heaven one day with the Lord Jesus, the Blessed Mother Mary, all the angels and saints, and our dead loved ones who have gone on to meet their maker in heaven.

SEPTEMBER 17, 1995

Early Sunday morning
12:48 A.M.

You may ask the question, how do we receive Christ into ourselves?

The first, and primary answer, for you and me, Grandpa, is through Holy Communion. In Holy Communion, we receive the body and blood, soul and divinity of Jesus Christ into our very being. This is the life of Christ in us. This is the grace of God in our very lives.

How can you and I, Grandpa, go about making this grace grow in us? Well, as Catholics, we know that good works, done in grace, help keep us in grace. So what is one constant good work we can do? Given the fact that, because of my mental illness, and your old age, Grandpa, we find ourselves housebound. The ANSWER: we can pray the rosary every day. Yes, just because we don't get out much, this does not stop us from saying the rosary every day. (I say mine at night.) This is our good work done in grace. It helps keep us in grace. We gain merit for this. This merit then leads to our salvation in heaven one day with God.

So Jesus changes us into presentable human beings. He makes us acceptable to the Father in heaven. He does this through the Sacrament of the Holy Eucharist. To have eternal life in us, we must eat the flesh of Jesus, and drink the blood of Jesus. We really and truly do this when we go to Communion. Me on Wednesday, you on Friday.

But we only go to Holy Communion once a week. This is why we must pray every day as a good work. The rosary is an excellent way of spending about a half hour a day in prayer with Jesus and the Blessed Mother Mary. This good work then keeps us in the grace of God, that comes through the Virgin Mary and our rosary.

The last thing I want to say is that you and I are without mortal sin. If ever we did get this type of sin, we would need God's forgiveness in the Sacrament of Confession. Both of us are in a state of grace. We do not need to go to Confession. We just want to receive more merit through good works done in grace. This is the rosary for us. We want more merit for a higher place in heaven, closer to Jesus and Mary.

SO WE NEED, DEEP DOWN INSIDE, THE HOLY EUCHARIST AND THE ROSARY!!!

SEPTEMBER 24, 1995

>Sunday, early morning
>1:11 A.M.

Dear Grandpa,

I am up late again at night. It is nice and quiet at this time of night. All the boys are in bed. David Sebastian will be getting up in an hour or two. He has a hard time sleeping because of depression. Right now I have the entire house to myself. After this letter is completed, it will be time for another load of tobacco in my pipe. I smoke "half and half" pipe tobacco prepared in individual pouches. Today it has been three whole weeks without a single cigarette in my mouth. This is good news for my lungs. But pipe tobacco is still not the most healthy thing to smoke. I do know that it is better health-wise than cigarettes. A pipe is also more dignified, and less punk-like in appearance. Seldom do I have the urge for a cigarette, as my pipe tobacco satisfies my craving for nicotine.

(If you wish to purchase any half and half tobacco for my birthday on January 4, 1996, when I come to your house, buy the 1 1/2 ounce pouches. This is what I mean by individual pouches.)

Also, to keep you up on what is going on here in the front room, Rob Parsons just got up to smoke a cigarette and eat some potato chips.

Everyone is back in bed now. It's just me, the typewriter, and classical music on the radio.

Let's talk about the Blessed Mother Mary now, in a poem.

Mary is our mother dear,
Who brought Jesus into the world.
He wipes away all our fear,
While far away the devil is hurled.

She held that little boy in her arms
And kissed him on his cheek;
For the devil this set off alarms,
Because to Jesus, the baby, she was so meek.

Then she saw the man upon a cross to die,
All the blood drained form his body.
'Twas there and then she did cry.
The devil is so shoddy.

But that old devil cannot keep Mary down,
For the Queen of Heaven is her name,
And she's known all over that holy town.
Let's hope for you and me one day, it's the same.

MARY
(This poem is given with respect, to Grandpa from David R. Wehner)

Her bare feet shod in sandals
One of them upon the serpent's head—
This done, by bringing the Redeemer into the world
To cast out the devil.

Her love we can feel from afar,
Warm and tender we do know,
For our mother Mary dear
Her son to us does show.

Upon a cross He did hang;
She was at its foot
While the angels sang,
"Come home to God Almighty, His Son."

On Pentecost Sunday, Mary did know
All the meaning of the cross for man,
Sharing with the apostles in the upper room
The Father's mighty plan.

So that old serpent upon his head she stands,
Knowing of God's eternal mind.
And to rescue man
Come to our aid, Mary, mother dear.

It is your Son who saves,
But for us you lead the way.
When the dead come forth from their graves,
Mary, the Queen of Heaven, will be there that day,

Clothed in the sunlight,
The moon at her feet,
Twelve stars, for the twelve apostles
Around her spiritually beautiful smiling face.

And the Lord our Redeemer,
His mother at His side
As they turn to one another,
Into heaven we will glide.

UNDATED (I)

Dear Grandpa,

At the Annunciation by the angel Gabriel, the Holy Spirit caused the Lord Jesus Christ to become conceived in the womb of the Virgin Mary. Then mother Mary left to see her cousin, Elizabeth, in the hill country. Elizabeth, seeing Mary, greeted her as the mother of Jesus. Soon came the birth of Jesus on that first Christmas morning. Mary and Joseph then soon went to present the child at the temple. Here Mary went through a purification ceremony after having given birth. And Simeon was able to lay eyes upon the Messiah before he, Simeon, would die. For Simeon had been told of this honor he would be granted by God. At the Passover, Mary, Joseph and Jesus had gone to the temple. In this same locale, Jesus was lost, in the temple. Here, as a young boy, He taught the wise men with authority. He was separated from His parents, becoming lost from them in the temple. What a relief Joseph and Mary had at finding the boy safe.

At the agony in the garden, Jesus said, "Father, if this cup may pass, but Thy will, not mine be done." Then the terrible scourging at the pillar. The crowning with thorns. The soldiers mocked Him. Jesus then had to carry the great weight of the cross to His place of execution. Simon of Cyrene, a strong young man, was pressed into this service. The great weight of the cross had been taken off His shoulders only to make sure He would die upon the cross. For then came the nails into the flesh, and His crucifixion upon that instrument of torture. He died with the sins of the world upon Him, saying, "Father, Father, why has Thou forsaken me?"

On Easter Sunday, three days later, Jesus rose from the dead. And from this we KNOW that He lives on today, and forever. It is our hope that we will live good lives, far away from mortal sin, and to one day live on forever in heaven with Him and mother Mary. Forty days later came His Ascension into heaven to sit at the right hand of the Father. From here the Father and Son sent the Holy Spirit down to Mary and the apostles. This is the beginning of the church. Jesus is still alive down here on earth today. Through His Spirit, the Spirit of Christ, the Holy Spirit. This is the Mystical Body of Christ, of which we are a part as Roman Catholics. At the end of Mary's life, she did not undergo the decay of the grave. Her Assumption then took place. Body and soul, she was taken up into heaven. Jesus showed HONOR to his mother by not letting her body know decay in the grave. He took her up into heaven for her Coronation, and she was made Queen of Heaven. And there she is today, forever Queen of Heaven, in union with the King of Kings, Jesus Christ our Lord.

MARY OF THE MIRACULOUS MEDAL

Dear mother Mary, fix your tender, loving, eyes upon us.
To look upon your poor children down here on this earth.
And then show to us your Son our Savior
As you intercede for all mankind.

We see the twinkle in your loving eyes,
And your smile, oh so dear.
Yes, the loving, sweet, smile of a mother
Who brings God's love so near.
Extend your arms and hands toward us,
For from them God's graces flow.
You are a great and mighty advocate
Bringing us ever closer to Christ the Lord.

On the back of the Miraculous Medal
The cross, and your letter "M," do combine.
And coming from this union
Are love and tender mercy for all humankind.

And the power of Christ the Lord
Does through you flow,
From the throne of heaven,
Giving God's graces to man below.

Where once was fear, now is love.
Gentle mother, you show the way
And lead us all the way to Jesus,
So far from Him we do not stray.

O Lord Jesus Christ, O Holy Blessed Mother,
You are together on the Miraculous Medal
And in heaven up above,
So to both of you we turn
For guidance, help, and love.

A TELEVISION SET IN EVERY AMERICAN HOME

I am a voice crying out in the wilderness,
But the people have ears of stone.
Yes, God's angel will pour out His vial of wrath.
Upon America will come many plagues.

Teenage pregnancy, drive-by shootings, and drug
    abuse,
these are but the surface of the plagues.
Homosexuality, and fornication and adultery between
men and women, are at the core of the great problem.
Television and Hollywood are the new gods of these
    End Times.

I am a voice crying out in the wilderness,
But the people have ears of stone.
All in the United States government seem corrupt,
Every politician grabbing for power.

Say anything, promise anything, give the people
more and more perversion.
Lust is the new main god of today—
The fruits of which are: abortion, adultery, and
homosexuality.
There seems to be no more the long enduring love of
a man and woman between themselves, as in bygone
    days.

So turn on your television set, vote for your favorite
politician, keep doing things the way everybody else
　　does.
Make sure you don't say a deep heartfelt prayer to
　　God.
Worship the sins of America.

I am a voice crying out in the wilderness,
But the people still have ears of stone.

OCTOBER 18, 1995

Dear Grandpa,
    Mary is our Mother dear,
    Bringing Jesus into the world.

    She is not only His one true mother,
    But in a very real and mystical way, our mother too.

    This is because she shows us her Son.
    To bring us, her children, closer to Him in heaven.
    She intercedes with her Son on our behalf.
    If we make it to heaven, she is most happy and joyous.

    She is our advocate with God.
    Father, Son, and Holy Spirit.
    She pleads our case for us.
    Yes, God wants to give us what we need,
    But because of our sin,
    We need help from Mary to receive the grace of God.

    The entire Communion of Saints,
    Those in purgatory, heaven, and earth,
    All those in Christ Jesus—
    We all come together in prayer.
    And the blessed Mother Mary
    Is the only one (other than God)
    Above all angels and men.

Yes, Mary pleads our case to God,
Father, Son, and Holy Spirit.

She does it for you and me, Grandpa.
She talks to Father, Son, and Holy Spirit,
For you and me, Grandpa.

GRACE, WORKS & MERIT

Going back to confession after being away from the church for years—here initial grace is a totally free gift, and has nothing to do with good works.

A long-time, good, holy, Catholic, who has for quite some time already been in a state of grace, will perform good works as a result of God's grace, and receive merit. It is grace, in this case, that does most of the work; but the individual's service to God is still important. The good works of this person help keep him close to God. And they help keep him living a grace-filled, Christ-like, existence. He receives merit for these good works. None of it would be possible without the grace of God. This individual wants to follow in the path of Jesus. He wants to do good works with the help of grace. These good works done in grace help keep him in a state of grace; they help to bring about a state of salvation.

Grace is, however, the essence of salvation. Even though the essence of salvation is grace, good works done in grace help keep one on the path of salvation. So, grace is the most important, but good works count too, because these good works done in grace bring about merit, which in the end, leads to salvation in heaven one day. I will say it again one more time. Good works done in Christ Jesus enable one to live a holy Christ-like existence here on earth. This is what one receives merit for. This merit then leads to salvation one day with Jesus and Mary in heaven. This is our joyful hope.

MARY

Mary was Immaculately Conceived without sin, in a "great favor" granted by God. Further, her body never knew decay in the grave, because of her Assumption, body and soul, into heaven. Jesus showed "honor" to His mother by not letting her body know the decay of the grave.

We honor Mary. She is a model of faith. Ever since she was small, and now, and for the rest of eternity—Mary did, and continues to, consent to God's will. With total obedience to God, and all her love, MARY CONSENTED TO THE CRUCIFIXION OF JESUS HER SON, knowing it was the will of God. Her heart was pierced with a sword, in the great good work done in grace. Now we can pray to Mary. She is in union with Jesus in heaven. She is the Queen of Heaven. We honor Mary. She leads us to Jesus Christ our Lord.

God's grace is the life of Jesus Christ, in a person. The good works, of this individual, done in grace, mean a Christ-like existence for him. He becomes a little Christ. He offers up his suffering and trials in this life, to God. It is this open willingness to suffer life's trials, that gives this individual a proper Christian attitude, and keeps him in a state of grace. It is a good work, done in grace, to offer up suffering. This good work keeps the individual in a state of grace. And grace is the life of Jesus Christ in this individual.

We must carry our cross in life. If we say no, then God will say no to the life of His Son in our soul. This yes, to willingly suffer, is an act of the will, and as such is a work, because it is a work of the mind. Life is full of suffering. We can fight it and curse God. Or we can humble ourselves, and willingly carry our own little cross in this life down here on earth. It brings the promise of heaven, where we will be with Jesus one day. All we need do is say yes to Him now.

UNDATED (II)

Dear Grandpa,
 In the early days of the church, the apostles and others helped to form the Catholic faith. The church, as time went on, put together the Bible. Now, today, the bishops and Pope John Paul II, bring us the word of God as stated in the Bible. (Sacred tradition is also a large part of our faith.) Jesus is alive in the church through its leaders. Also, we as good, conservative Catholics, are members of the Body of Christ. But we must never forget that we must follow the holy teachings of the Pope and his bishops.
 I find in my life that, through the communion of saints, Father Ken Graham (who died three and a half years ago) comes into my heart and soul with the grace of Jesus Christ our Lord. (Also, my praying of the rosary every night in my room is a great comfort to me. It is a source of spiritual strength and renewal daily.) All I need to do to have peace of mind is to reflect upon the past words of Father Graham. He said those words to me mostly in the sacrament of confession, to which I went to him with a repentant heart, some thirty-five times, for the last one and a half years of Father's life here on earth. This took place at the Menlo Park Veterans Hospital chapel, where Father Graham was the Catholic chaplain.
 I am currently reading a book called *The Privilege of Being Catholic*. Father Oscar Lukefahr is the author. Father Oscar and I correspond through the U.S. mail. He has helped me a

great deal in his book, and in his individual letters to me. Father Oscar keeps the spirit of Father Graham alive to me through his letters and book.

Jesus Christ our Lord comes to me every Wednesday morning at 10:30 A.M. when Jack Youngs, a Eucharistic minister, brings me Holy Communion. This, of course, it goes without saying, is the source of all my spiritual strength. Jesus Christ the Lord made alive to me, Body and Blood, Soul and Divinity, in the Holy Eucharist.

I am very fortunate to be Catholic. To be in a religion that is true to God's word, as it was put down in the beginning by Jesus Christ. The writers of the Old Testament were inspired by the Holy Spirit. The writers of the New Testament—some of them—knew Jesus while He was on earth. The Catholic church by the year 300 decided on which books would be in the Old and New Testament. In 1546 the Council of Trent said the Alexandrian (Christian) Old Testament would stand. And they reaffirmed the traditional list of New Testament books. And these teachings are passed on to us as Catholics through the Vicar of Christ, Pope John Paul II. He stands in on earth for Jesus Christ our Lord.

I am very happy to be a good, conservative, Roman Catholic lay person. My faith means the world to me. I will take it with me to my grave. And be joyous doing this.

MARY, OUR LIFE
(October 25, 1995)

You are our LIFE, dear mother Mary.
Because the Son of God, Jesus Christ, was brought to
    this world
By your yes to God the Father Almighty.
Without your yes (which was preordained from the
    beginning
Of time, and although you had a free will to say no)
There would have been no Redeemer.
So in this very important way you are our LIFE,
Dear mother Mary.
Because you are the mother of God, you have been
    given
A position in heaven just below the throne of God,
Father, Son, and Holy Spirit,
Where you are in union with Jesus Christ the Lord,
The Son of God the Father,
And your Son too.
From your throne, just below God's throne, as Queen
    of Heaven,
You dispense all God's graces to mankind as the
    mother of God.
In that God's grace flows through you, dear mother
    Mary,
And that you are our advocate at God's throne,
You are our LIFE, and our hope, dear mother Mary.

You are our way to God.
You are our way to LIFE.

You are truly the mother of God,
And our mother too.

O sweet, loving, Virgin Mary,
Keep us in the graces of God.
Through yourself let pass to us the Holy Spirit,
The Spirit of Jesus Christ the Lord,
To us your poor children down in this valley of tears.

God knows about everything we need.
Mary goes to Him on our behalf,
Because we have some sins that keep us from making good contact.
Once she makes contact with God for us,
He sends us His grace through her.
This allows us to become better Catholics in this grace.
We open ourselves to God's grace in this way.
We seek to model our lives after the life of Mary.
The more we do this, the more we open ourselves to God's grace.

In the final analysis, it is up to us to amend our lives,
And actually live a Christ-like existence in this world.
God the Father Almighty wants all of us to do this.
And He gives us all the grace we need to accomplish this task.
Even as we become more saintly, we still must remain humble,
Realizing we still need Mary's help as an advocate to God.

We are never free from all venial sin.
This is why we always need her help in seeking God.

She stands in at His throne on our behalf.
Jesus sees His perfect mother requesting that aid and
 help come our way.
He is moved to help us.
Then we are moved to become more like Jesus Christ
 the Lord,
And His mother the Virgin Mary, in our lives.
God knows everything we need.
We just need a little help from our Lady as an
 advocate to receive it.
The real burden of changing one's life is still up to
 that individual.
So we truly must become good, holy Catholics in the
 truest sense of these words.
God is not going to wave a magic wand for us.
We must do some real hard work to become good
 Catholics.
But God in His mercy has already realized how hard
 it is for
Us to get started, because of our sins,
So He has given us His mother the Virgin Mary as an
 advocate,
So we must pick up the pieces of our lives and go to
 work,
Doing our utmost to become good, holy Catholics.
Mary is a starting point, and our finishing point in
 heaven

Is also with her—
With her and her Son—
Both of whom are waiting in heaven for us.

Both of whom are waiting in heaven for us.

Our aid then comes from the Blessed Mother Mary.
She is the dispenser of all God's graces—
And everything in everything of all our hopes and
 fears.
The totality of our lives comes from God,
Father, Son, and Holy Spirit.
Mary is our avenue to this hoped-for rendezvous
 with God in heaven.
Jesus Christ her Son is whom she shows to us in her
 every prayer.

NOVEMBER 11, 1995

Veteran's Day

Dear Grandpa,

We look devoutly on, or venerate, all that is in heaven with God. Father, Son, and Holy Spirit are the only God we worship.

In order of importance, starting with number one. We worship God alone. Then we "venerate" the Blessed Virgin Mary, the mother of God. We also venerate all the angels of heaven. The twelve apostles are to be venerated. And lastly, we venerate all the saints.

We look with love upon our dead loved ones who died in Christ Jesus, and are now in heaven with Him. Also, we look with love upon the poor souls in purgatory. They too can intercede with God for us, because they are in a state of grace, for they only died with venial sins on their souls. Or they did not suffer enough down here on earth to pass purgatory by.

As to all human beings on this earth, we look at them as being made in the image and likeness of God. As we treat any man or woman, boy or girl, in this world, so we treat Jesus Christ our Lord. We must show love to our brothers and sisters in this world. This is how we make it to heaven in the next world with Jesus Christ and the Blessed Mother Mary, and all the angels and saints. Not to leave out our dead loved ones. They are waiting for us on the other side of life, too. They are in heaven or purgatory. It does not matter where. Because from both places they end up in heaven with God, and with all of heaven there, too.

WHAT WE SHARE WITH JESUS

We can do nothing apart from Jesus. He conquered sin on the Cross. We make up our minds not to sin, but we are only able to avoid sin through joining with Jesus. It is he working in us, who brings about obedience.

We gain some merit in carrying our own cross. That is, we are all little individual Christs. And by faith, in our own little way, we share in the Cross of Jesus. We do this with Him, not apart from Him. There is merit in suffering, in being like Jesus.

Also, charity towards our neighbor gives us merit. We join with Jesus, and forgive others. Almsgiving to the poor gains us merit. This is bearing fruit. These are the works of our faith. We can pray for the poor souls in purgatory. A good way to say the rosary. We can ask Jesus and Mary to watch over the people of the world. And most of all to believe in Jesus. To have faith in Him. We love what we have faith in, and we don't want to commit any mortal sins. Jesus says, if you love me, you will keep my commandments. When we fall into mortal sin, then we must go to confession. We want to stay in a state of grace. We want to love Jesus, not drive the nail deeper into his hand. O Mary, conceived without sin, pray for us, who have recourse to thee.

We not only share in the suffering of Jesus. We also share in His peace. We gain merit and peace when we help others. We help them make it in life, and get to heaven in the next life. This is the work of Jesus. To suffer with Him. To share in His Peace. To unite our own suffering with His Cross. To have peace of mind in obedience (avoiding sin) and good works.

MARY IS OUR HOPE JESUS OUR SALVATION

As Catholics, in our faith we believe in the death and resurrection of Jesus Christ, our Lord and Savior. We need to live this faith. Faith without works is dead. We want to pick up our cross and carry it. Our master picked up His cross. We must do the work of Jesus here on earth to make it a better place. And with the help of the Holy Spirit, we are able to perform good works of our own free will through the free loving gift of the grace of God. These good works done in grace become meritorious of heaven one day, because it is by living an existence patterned after that of Jesus that we meet God. He supplies the grace; we supply the faith, and the works. Religion is life. And life is works. We must live a good, holy, religious life if we wish to make it to heaven.

It is through the good works and prayers of our faith that we have faith, that we live our faith. We must live our faith. Jesus did. Mary did. Many good Catholics do this very thing every day.

Mary is our hope. Jesus is our salvation. She is His mother. He was born of a virgin. She stood at the foot of the cross. He hung upon it. By the power of God, she was taken up into heaven, body and soul. His resurrection from the grave was brought about through the power of God the Father Almighty. Her coronation makes her Queen of Heaven. He is Jesus Christ, the King of Kings. She is the queen mother, who intercedes to His throne for us. He grants His mother's every prayer. For us, Mary is the way to Christ, our Lord in heaven. His Spirit, the Holy Spirit, can be in our hearts. Mary is a way through her intercession to receive the grace of the Spirit. Jesus wants to be our friend and live in our hearts and souls. Mary intercedes with her Son to help bring this about.

We honor Mary. She is a model of faith. She is a guide to Jesus and His truth. Ever since she was small, and now, and for the rest of eternity—Mary did, and continues to, consent to God's will. With total obedience to God and all her love, Mary consented to being the mother of God, knowing it was the will of God the Father.

Mary also consented to the crucifixion of Jesus. Her heart was pierced with a sword in the great good work of her will done in grace. Now we can pray to Mary as the Mother of God. We can also know she was at the foot of the cross. She is now in union with Jesus in heaven. She is the Queen of Heaven.

We honor Mary. She is a mother who saw her Son born, and then die on a cross; and then she soon knew of His resurrection from the grave. Mary leads us to Jesus Christ our Lord.

IMMACULATE CONCEPTION

O Mary conceived without sin, pray for us who have recourse (turn) to thee.

With these holy words, we can look back to the eleventh century in the Western church. Here is the early beginning, in the West, of the doctrine of the Immaculate Conception. This was the Catholic church in England at the time. Even earlier, this same doctrine started to surface in the East. This was in the seventh century. This is the earliest beginning of this doctrine.

Later in 1308, Duns Scotus said Christ can save in two ways. The main way was through His death upon the cross after the fact. Mary was preserved from ever being touched by sin, even for an instant. This was done through the foreseen merits of Jesus. Thus, the Immaculate Conception. Pope Pius IX on December 8, 1854 created the feast day. Prior to this, Saint Catherine Laboure had a vision of Mary in 1830 through which we received the Miraculous Medal. This is also known as the medal of the Immaculate Conception, because of the words that are written on the medal.

O Mary, your medal protects us. We wear it close to our hearts. It reminds us of your love, the love of a mother for her children. You don't want us to end up outside the love of God, so when we turn to you, we receive God's grace through you.

All we need do to receive this grace is: live a good, strict, conservative Catholic life. And go to confession when we need it. A good priest can help us. With all this comes the most important thing: when you show us your Son Jesus, dear Mary.

MARY, A WAY TO JESUS AND HEAVEN

Soon after the birth of our Lord Jesus,
A few hundred years,
Mary was honored by the Church
As the mother of God.

In the seventh century in the East
And the eleventh century in the West,
Was celebrated the Immaculate Conception of Mary.
Pius IX in 1854 made it a Holy Day of Obligation.

In 1950 Pius XII declared the Feast of the Assumption,
When Mary was taken up body and soul into heaven.
This was done through God in Jesus Christ
To show honor to His mother.

Today all Catholics honor Mary as mother of God.
Jesus then puts it in our hearts to receive Holy
    Communion,
His body and blood in the form of bread and wine.
This is the summit of our faith, the Holy Eucharist.

For many Catholics it all starts with love for Mary.
Gently she guides us to her Son,
With the loving touch of a mother,
Until that day that we stand before Him to be judged.

Mother Mary will tell Him
"This is my child,
A child who followed your way, my Son,
So please, my Lord, into your kingdom do take him."

And Jesus will say,
"Upon the earth you partook of my body and blood.
Eternal life you now have.
Here in my kingdom, with my mother and Me."

And all of the while
It was Mary's guiding hand
That had led us to heaven
In front of our Savior to stand.

MARY STOOD AT THE FOOT OF THE CROSS

Mary stood at the foot of the cross
With the disciple Jesus loved.
Jesus said, "Woman, here is your son."
Then He said to the disciple,
"Here is your mother."
This use of the word *woman* invites a deeper meaning,
In that it is a reference to Eve,
For Jesus told the serpent in the garden:
"I will put enmity between you and the woman,
And between your offspring and hers;
He will strike your head,
And you will strike his heel."

Yes, Mary stood at the foot of the cross.
She saw her Son die on that cross.
But in the death and resurrection of Jesus,
He dealt a death blow to Satan
So Mary is the new Eve,
The mother of all who believe in Jesus,
And who are obedient to His commands.
She lovingly consented to the death of her Son upon
 the cross.
Being obedient to God,
We Catholics are to do the same.

O Virgin Daughter of Zion,

Show us the way to your Son,
Our Lord Jesus Christ.
Teach us by example to be obedient unto Him.
He died that we may live.
He rose from the dead
That we may share in His glory one day in heaven.
You too were taken up into heaven in His glory.
Thus we Catholics believe in your Assumption.
If we believe,
And if we are good,
One day at the end of the world
Our souls will join what will then be our glorified bodies.
Your Son has paved the way to heaven for us.
O Virgin Daughter of Zion,
You are a model of how to arrive there in heaven one day.
You will then show us the blessed fruit of your womb,
JESUS.

FOUR CATHOLIC DOGMAS ABOUT THE VIRGIN MARY

January 10th, 1996

1. At her birth she was Immaculately Conceived without any sin whatsoever. The Cross of Jesus Christ brought about Mary's Immaculate Conception, before Jesus actually hung on the cross. By the *grace of God*, this took place, for Mary, before the crucifixion.
2. The Annunciation points explicitly to the fact that Mary was a virgin long before, and after becoming pregnant, with Jesus. It also implies that she remained ever a virgin. This was done so that Mary and Joseph could totally concentrate on their son Jesus, the Son of God. One can see that with such a holy responsibility, Mary and Joseph would give up their pleasure together in order to be completely spiritually tuned into Jesus Christ our Lord and their Lord.
3. The divine motherhood of Mary is celebrated on January 1st. The feast is called "Mary Mother of God." This is the greatest single act of Mary's life, that is saying "yes" to being the mother of God.
4. The feast of the Assumption of the Blessed Virgin Mary. Mary is taken up to heaven. She is given the same type of glorified body her son Jesus had at His Ascension. *On the last day,* our bodies will also be glorified like Mary's through Jesus Christ our Lord's power, grace, and mighty love for us. Mary leads the way to

Jesus and heaven for us. As the mother of God, Jesus honored his own mother by not letting her body know decay.

GRACE

In Baptism we receive free God-given grace.
This grace extends throughout our entire life.
However, mortal sin will remove all of God's grace
  from us.
To regain grace we repent of our mortal sin in
  Confession.
If we are true to the life of Jesus Christ in us,
then we will develop grace in our life.
This is done primarily through the Sacraments,
especially the Holy Eucharist,
For this is the very Body and Blood of our Savior
Jesus Christ.
In this holy meal, just as at the Last Supper,
we take our Lord Jesus into our own body.
Here His will is made known to our human minds.

As a result of grace from the Sacraments, especially
Communion and Confession, we live holy lives.
We use our free will to choose to serve God.
We also use our will to follow the teachings of the
Church, and those of Jesus in the Bible.
We may seek, at this time, to raise our children better.
Or as I do, to pray the rosary for my family,
as I am single, and have no children.
Good works of this nature help keep us in the grace
  of God—

That is, God's grace makes the good works possible,
and then elevates them to a stature where they
are meritorious.

It all starts with the free God-given grace of Baptism.
From this grace comes the will to serve others,
And to do our best to help bring about our own
 salvation,
and the salvation of others,
such as those in our families.
Jesus Christ is our Lord and Savior.
The best of all ways to find Him, and therefore His
 grace,
is through the Holy Eucharist of the Roman Catholic
 Church.
Here Jesus comes down from heaven with all His love
to live in our hearts.

We believe that the Body and Blood of Jesus Christ
are present in the bread and wine.
This is done through the power of God.
It is, however, a matter of faith on our part that we
believe this.
More precisely, it is through this belief that we are
 saved—
This, as we take God into our own body in the form of
Communion.

If we lose this grace to mortal sin, the sacrament of
confession will restore it.
Here the blood of Jesus that was shed upon the cross
wipes away all our sin.
This is a free gift, this forgiveness.
We do not earn it.

It comes through faith in the cross, and sorrow for sin.

All we need then is: FAITH to receive the Grace of
   God.
And sorrow for sin.
And the real presence of Jesus in Communion.
And the priest standing in for Jesus in the
   confessional.
Then we are saved through Jesus Christ our Lord.

TIME TRANSCENDED IN A MIRACLE

God Almighty, through the power of Jesus Christ, brought
about the Immaculate Conception of the Blessed Virgin Mary.
How, you ask, was this done before the life, death, and
resurrection of Jesus Christ?
It is possible because God is not hemmed in by the limits of time and
space.
He therefore kept Mary free from all stain of sin even before His
saving mission down here on earth.

So, as Mary wears a crown of glory in heaven today,
it can be said that Jesus wore a crown of thorns,
for His mother Mary, even before she was Immaculately
Conceived in the womb of Saint Ann,
and that He died on the cross, and rose from the dead,
not limited by time and space, for His mother Mary.
And because He was not limited by time and space,
He died and rose for her in her Immaculate Conception,
thus setting His mother free from all stain of sin
for all time.

The rest of us are led to the cross of Jesus Christ by
the one who was at the foot of the cross as the mother
of God.
O Mother Mary, we love you.
You showed great love for your Son our Savior.
You show much great love for us, your children
down here
on earth, too.
Keep us in the grace of God, dear virgin mother Mary.
We honor you, because you teach us to worship your
Son,
our Lord and Savior Jesus Christ.

JANUARY 21, 1996

At the Annunciation the angel Gabriel proclaimed to Mary: "Hail Mary, full of grace, the Lord is with thee." Here God is showering His favor upon Mary by making her full of grace by being with her. God is preparing Mary to say yes to being the mother of His Son, Jesus. The incarnation of Jesus will happen when Mary says: "Be it done unto me according to thy word." She went to see her cousin Elizabeth who was six months pregnant with John the Baptist. Mary greeted Elizabeth at the home of Zacharius, the husband of Elizabeth. Upon Mary's words to Elizabeth, Elizabeth said as the Holy Spirit came upon her, "Blessed art thou among women, and blessed is the fruit of thy womb, Jesus." Again Mary knew God had done a great work in her life.

Then the Baby Jesus was born in a manger. The shepherds came, there was the star of Bethlehem, and the three wise men came to see the boy, King Jesus. All this had been foretold in the Old Testament. Surely, Mary knew a great thing had been accomplished in her. Then the baby Jesus was presented at the Temple in Jerusalem. Here Simeon told Mary that her heart would be pierced with a sword. And it soon happened. King Herod tried to kill baby Jesus. Mary had to move to the faraway land of Egypt, leaving all her friends behind. This was a rocky road for Mary and Joseph. Mary kept her faith through all these trials. At the age of twelve, the boy Jesus was lost in the Temple. When Mary and Joseph finally found Him teaching the wise men in the

Temple days later, they were relieved a great deal. Jesus said to Mary and Joseph a short kind of statement. "Do you not know I must be about my Father's business." Mary did not become angry. Only the Father in heaven knew everything about Jesus. Mary therefore was taken a bit back by this statement. But Mary kept her cool. Even though she did not know everything about Jesus, she did not sin even in the slightest degree. She is the perfect mother. But she had plenty of tests of her faith during her whole life.

Now we find Mary at the foot of the cross. Her son is dead. Still she keeps all her faith. She kept trusting in God. She kept trusting even when all looked black, as if God the Father Almighty had turned His back on her. Then Mary heard news of the Resurrection. This was the reward that was to come to her. Then the Ascension of Jesus. Later on Pentecost Sunday, Mary and the Apostles received the Holy Spirit. Here Mary was given real Joy and Peace in her heart. It did not mean that she had a life with no troubles. But it did mean she knew completely, that her Son was the second person of the Trinity, the Son of God, Jesus Christ the Lord. Finally came Mary's Assumption, when her body and soul were glorified like those of Jesus. Then her Coronation in heaven, where she sits today on her own high place near Father, Son, and Holy Spirit. The Queen of Heaven, queen of the angels, Queen of the Apostles, Queen of the Saints, and queen of all the loved ones who have gone on before us in Christ Jesus. WE CAN REACH JESUS THROUGH MARY. SHE SHOWS US THE WAY TO HER SON BY THE LIFE SHE LED DOWN HERE ON EARTH. MOTHER MARY, JESUS CHRIST, GOD THE FATHER, HOLY SPIRIT, ME AND GRANDPA LOVE YOU.

JANUARY 27, 1996

Dear Dad and Dear Grandpa,
   Yes we can pray directly to Mary. This is evident in the prayer written on the Miraculous Medal. "O Mary, conceived without sin, pray for recourse to thee." It can also be prayed: "O Mary, conceived without turn to thee."

   Mary gave this prayer to Saint Catherine Laboure. It comes directly from heaven. This is not a matter of church dogma. But there have been many miracles associated with the Miraculous Medal. You can't tell the people like me who wear it that they do not receive protection from Our Lady. Of course this is done through the power of Jesus Christ.

   I have been praying the rosary for about seven months now, every day. I pray directly to Mary when I pray my rosary. Mary is the queen mother. She has the ear of the King Jesus Christ. We can go directly to her in prayer, in that she is seated on a throne as Queen of Heaven, next to her Son Jesus, the Father, and the Holy Spirit of God surrounds them, and surrounds all of heaven and earth. Mary is a way to Jesus, and therefore a way to God Almighty Himself.

   Bonnie, this letter is also for my dad, along with Grandpa. That is why I put dear dad, and dear grandpa at the top of this page.

JESUS, ALWAYS PRESENT IN OUR LIVES

We find Jesus in Holy Communion. This is the risen glorified Christ. At this time He comes into our hearts. The bread is His body. The wine is His blood. A body that died on the cross for us. And blood that was shed so we can be forgiven. This is in our memory at the time of Holy Communion. Jesus is very much alive in communion. Our will is one with His will at this time. We feel His real presence. We receive the ability and blessing at this time to receive Holy Communion, to live our lives for Jesus.

God loves us. He wants to show us this. This life is hard. God can give us a reason to live. He can make the depression and hard times make some sense. This is because we know if we stick it out with Him until the end, we will end up in heaven.

"Holy Mary, mother of God," we pray. "Ask your Son, the Son of God, to send us His Spirit, the Holy Spirit. Let us rejoice with Him, Let us suffer with Him here on earth, and one day be with Him in heaven."

Jesus is the perfect sacrifice upon the cross. It is only because of Him that our sins are forgiven. Mary and mankind add their own suffering to the perfect sufferings of Jesus. We do this when we pass through the trials and tribulations. We know we have a friend in Jesus. And also in Mary. They suffer along with us, as we offer up our suffering, as we carry our own cross.

God the Father Almighty, the cross of Jesus, and the

grace of the Holy Spirit, and the Blessed Mother Mary, are in the center of heaven. They are surrounded by all the angels, the twelve apostles, and all the other saints. This is the glory of God.

FEBRUARY 13, 1996

Dear Grandpa,
 In a mystical communion through Jesus Christ our Lord, and the indwelling of the Holy Spirit in our hearts, through this, the Blessed Virgin Mary, all the angels and saints, and the whole host of heaven, along with our loved ones who have passed on in Christ Jesus, through this Jesus Christ our Lord brings the love that all of heaven has for Him into our hearts and souls.
All my love,
David